YouTube Marketing

A Comprehensive Guide for Building Authority, Creating Engagement and Making Money Through Facebook

Mark Smith

Table of Contents

Introduction

Congratulations on downloading this book and thank you for doing so.

The following chapters will discuss some of the basics that you need to know in order to get started with YouTube marketing. This is a form of marketing that some companies tend to overlook, but it is one of the best options that you can use to really form a relationship with your customers and promote your business. This book is going to spend some time talking about how to get started on YouTube marketing for your business.

There are so many things that you can do with YouTube that it is simply amazing. You don't want to just get started right away with a whole bunch of videos that will just talk about the product all the time. There is no connection here and your potential customers will get bored and quit following you. This book will not only show you how to make these sales videos later on down the line, but how to work on those first few videos so that you really impress the viewers and get them to stick around.

We will also talk about how you can provide value to your audience, how to really make those videos and the front page of your channel pop out, how to use analytics to figure out how well your videos are doing, and even how AdWords will help you to promote your site better than ever before. When all of these parts come together, it is really easy for you to get the views, and even the sales, that you would like.

When you are ready to see your business grow and you want to start adding some marketing with YouTube to the mix, make sure to check out this book. It has all the information that you need to make the right decisions and see an increase in sales in no time.

There are plenty of books on this subject on the market, thanks again for choosing this one! Every effort was made to ensure it is full of as much useful information as possible, please enjoy!

Chapter 1: Getting Started with YouTube

Before we start looking at some of the cool marketing things that you can do with YouTube, it is important to get a good look at how YouTube works and how it got its start. This platform has such a huge audience with more than 800 million active users each month. This makes it the number one destination for browsing, searching, sharing, and promoting video content. When people want to see a video of something, whether it is about cooking, working out, how things are done, and so on, they are going to head to YouTube.

This means that YouTube is one of the most effective platforms that you can use to build up a big group of loyal followers, which are known as subscribers on this platform. Unlike some of the other social media platforms, like Facebook and Instagram, all the content that is placed on YouTube is going to be in a video format, making it very unique and personal.

Now, when it comes to marketing on YouTube, there are three pillars that are very critical. The first pillar is that you need to attract an audience to your channel through the videos you post. The better your videos, the more followers you will get. The second pillar is that you need to engage the audience. Your audience needs to have some kind of involvement, emotionally or otherwise, with you or they will stop visiting. And the third pillar is that you need to upsell to your audience, which means that you should sell some kind of service or product to your audience.

All of these parts need to come together, through the videos that you create in order to help you to get the followers and the profit that you want. Now, some people may already have a business that has been successful on other social media platforms and now they want to move it to YouTube. You will be able to use these videos to promote your product, just make sure that the videos are not too full of sales, that they have some kind of hook that brings customers in, or you will lose out.

In other cases, you may be brand new to the business and want to promote yourself or get the business off the ground. This is just fine as well, you just have to find your angle as well. Remember that it is all about the connection that you make with the audience. There are millions of videos on YouTube so you need to figure out what will draw in your customers? What will make them pick you over another video and what will keep them coming back for more? Yes, it is fine to advertise your product and this is a great way to promote your company, but this can get stale and boring if it is all you show your customers.

So, let's say that you are ready to get going on YouTube. There are a few things that you should have in order first. First, you need to set up an account. This is pretty easy to do. If you already have a Gmail account, you should have it linked to YouTube and can use the same credentials to log on. If your email is already professional and you are comfortable using this to promote your business, you will be able to go onto your account and start.

Since most people have a personal email address and they want to use YouTube to promote their business, they may want to consider setting up a unique email address that is just for their business or just on this YouTube channel. This is pretty easy to set up. You simply need to go to gmail.com and set up the email and password that you want to use. From there, go through and get onto your YouTube channel to start.

From here you can set up some of your own settings. You can choose what language you use, some of the keywords that come with your channel, and even how you receive notifications. And of course, take the time to post a few videos to get the channel started (we will discuss how to get those first videos going and what needs to be in your video to make it stand out).

YouTube is a great place to form a connection with your customers and to make sure that you are able to sell your product in a way that other social media platforms are not able to do. This book will give you the answers that you need to get started and really build up that following in no time.

Benefits of marketing with YouTube

At this point, you may be wondering why you should take the time to market on YouTube. There are a lot of other sources for advertising that you can consider, so why would YouTube be one of the options that you put on your list. There are actually the number of reasons why YouTube can work so well, sometimes way better than the other avenues, and this can be true no matter what type of product or service you are trying to sell. Some of the benefits of working on YouTube include:

- It's free: while you will need to invest a bit of your time to figure out your target audience and to create the videos that you want to use, being able to upload and even make the videos that you want to upload will be completely free. What is another advertising source going to be free?

- Content is really powerful: in a world that is moving more and more online, content is king. And out of all this content, video content is some of the best. Many times people would rather watch information about a product or service online rather than read about it.
- Could go viral: if you make a video that is particularly good, emotional, funny, or something else, your video could have the potential to go viral in no time. What going viral means is that there could be thousands of people who will share your video with others they know. If it does really well, this could mean that your business is exposed to an infinite amount of people.
- Local and global audience: based on the types of keywords that you use, your video could be seen by people all over the world. You could even end up with clients from other countries if it all goes well. If you are worried about the reach going too far because you are just a local business, it is possible to change this so that you are only found by people in your region.
- Demonstrate your expertise: you can spend your videos giving away great tips, which help to show your viewers that you are the expert in your particular field. For many customers or clients that you are going after, they will have a choice between two businesses and you want to make sure that they pick you. If you have videos on YouTube that show why you are a good choice, this will help your business to stand out.
- Selling all the time: just because you just spend a little bit of time on a video and then post it doesn't mean the work your video is doing is all done. Making a video is like one of the best salespeople in the world. You only have to make the video once and then load it to YouTube. Then the video can go to work, being available any time of the day or night that someone wants to take

a look at it. And for each new video you create, you are making a new salesperson. There is really no limit to what you can do with this.

- Give them a face: sometimes what you need is to provide the customer with a face, a person they can trust, in order to form that connection to make the sale. And since it is impossible for you to go out there and meet all of your customers, creating a video that can do this work for you can really help If you are camera shy, you can make a video that is in PowerPoint and then add in a headshot so people can still see how you look.
- The video is very SEO friendly: this one is so important. When someone is doing a search online, it is likely that a video is going to hold onto a top spot during the organic searches. If this ends up being your video, this is a big deal because for one reason or another, and your hard work, your video is standing out above the other links. And of course, more people are going to see your video if it is ranked high in search results.

When it comes to marketing your business, there really isn't a site that is better than working with YouTube. This website will allow you to make some content that will connect with the customers and if you do the process right, which we will discuss more in later chapters, you are going to get some of the best conversion rates and sales ever.

Creating videos that do well

Of course, if you want to see some success on YouTube and do well, you need to make sure that you are creating some videos that will be popular on YouTube. Creating a good video can be tough. Some of the most popular videos that are available on this channel aren't particularly high quality, even though this is a feature that is recommended inside of your YouTube video, and some aren't all that unique. But they are still providing something of entertainment or value to the customer and so they are able to get a lot of views.

There are a few different factors that need to come into play when you create a video that is going to do well. You need to start out with a video that is high-quality as these are often going to do the best when you are working on a channel for your product or service. Try to make good videography, or hire someone who can, to help you get this.

You also need to add some value to the video. There needs to be some reason why people are going to choose to go with your video, and sit through and watch the whole thing, rather than moving on to something else. You need to be able to provide this value to your customers as much as possible. Figuring out how to add the value is the tough part since each company and product is going to be a bit different.

And you need to promote the video. If no one ever gets a chance to see your video because it gets lost on YouTube, it is going to be really hard to see your company do well. There are a few different methods of promotion that you are able to use, from AdWords and more.

Picking out keywords

While you work on your videos, you should be careful about the keywords that you use. This is going to be the best way to make sure that people are able to find your video when they are looking up topics similar to yours. There are many great keywords that you can choose from and pick the right ones can help you to find more viewers.

You should consider some of the things that your potential customers will look for when they need your product or service. What do the clients like to look up or what interests them the most? This is going to help you out quite a bit because it ensures that you are able to get the viewers that matter the most for you.

If you are not certain about which types of keywords you should use, think about
What is important to your users. There are also tools that you are able to use that help you pick out some of the best keywords. These really help you to reach your customers and get the viewers that you would like.

Adding value to the clients

No matter what kind of product you are selling or target audience you are trying to reach, you need to make sure that every video you create is adding some value to your customers. It is easy for someone who is new to the market to worry just about their own profits and making money, but if this kind of attitude starts to show up in your videos, and it will, you will never be able to get customers.

Your work should always be about what is best for the customer and one way to do this is to show the value of some kind to the customer. Even the videos that you do before you promote your product or service should be valuable to the customer. This can include entertainment value as well. If there isn't value to the customer in some way, they will not be willing to purchase it.

This is also where some of the relationship and connection between you and the customer will come into the picture. You want to create some videos that are going to not only do well but ones that help the customer feel like they are gaining value and becoming closer to you. When this happens they are much more likely to want to make a purchase from you later on when you start your conversion videos.

There are a lot of different ways that you are able to add some value to your customers. You can provide them with some entertainment value, something that will make them laugh or help them to feel emotional over your story. You can show them how the product will provide them some value in their daily lives (not just how the product works itself). Take a look at your product and some of the messages that you are trying to send out to the world, and you will be able to figure out the best way that your product is able to provide value to others.

Don't forget the promotion

You may have made the best YouTube video in the world, but without some promotion, it is unlikely that more than a few people are going to even look at the video You need to put in some effort to make a promotion work if you want to make some sales. The good news about YouTube is that there are millions of active viewers each month which means there are a lot of potentials. But it also means that there is going to be a lot of competition and if you don't do some promotion to help make your video stand out, it is going to end up lost in the crowd.

Since Google acquired YouTube recently, you will get the benefits of being able to use AdWords for Video to help you with this type of promotion. This is one of the best marketing and promotion tools that you can choose from. It has all the tools and you will be able to personalize things to reach the right target market, to stay within budget, and so much more. We will spend some more time talking about what AdWords is all about and even how to set up your own account.

You should really put this promotion to good use. Programs, especially AdWords, will be able to provide you with detailed information so you can see whether your work is paying off. You can see if you are reaching the right target market if you are seeing the conversion rates that you want and more. Never underestimate how these tools can work for you and use them to your full advantage.

No matter what kind of campaign you are trying to create, you need to use AdWords for Video on YouTube. But there are a few other methods that you can try out as well. Some people like to post their videos on Facebook. This is a good way to get some views because you can share with your friends and family, and ask them to share. If the video ends up being really good, you may end up with a video that goes viral.

Promotion is so important to help you see the results that you want with your video. Creating a marketing campaign can be a little bit scary, but it is the only way to figure out who you are advertising to and to make sure that your information is getting out to as many people as possible. There are a tons of great videos on YouTube that have never gotten any views before simply because the creators were too scared to run the promotion that they needed.

How well are you doing?

No matter what kind of product or service you are offering to other people, you need to make sure that you have some method in place that will help you determine if you are being successful or not. It is not good enough to just guess about this part because often you are going to be completely wrong. And since YouTube does have an analytics service available, why would you want to leave all of this to just guessing.

YouTube analytics will help you to keep track of what you are doing with your advertisements. You want to make sure that you are sending out the right message, that you are reaching the right kinds of people who would like to purchase your products and you want to make an impact with all of your hard work Using a tool like YouTube Analytics will help to make this happen.

There are quite a few options that you are able to choose when it comes to working on a marketing plan for your company. You can choose to work on advertising in print, radio, television, and even other social media sites. But nothing is as effective and unique as working with YouTube. This social media site will allow you to post videos, which really work in a unique way because they form a connection with you and the customer, something that is not always seen or possible with some of the other forms of advertisement that you want to work with. If you want to do something that is completely unique to your marketing campaign and reach a large group of people who will be interested in purchasing your products, it is time to start working on your very own YouTube campaign.

Chapter 2: Doing Your First Video

One of the biggest challenges that new marketers are going to face is to get new users to their channel and looking at their videos. There are millions of videos on YouTube so standing out in the crowd can seem really hard at times. You need to be able to create a video that not only sells your market and your product but which will really attract people to view your videos.

So how are you going to make sure that these potential customers see your videos and find them in the crowd on YouTube? The answer to getting through this problem is to do traffic videos. These are developed, and then uploaded, by the content creators and they are able to reach a lot of customers in a short amount of time. The main purpose of these videos is to bring as many people into your channel so that they can see your value and the main content that you want to show to them.

These videos can be powerful because it will set the tone for your whole channel. These videos are going to be pretty short though; most of them will not be more than seven minutes long. They will appeal to a lot of people so the views will be high, but remember that these videos are not going to speak to everyone and only a few of these viewers are going to become your subscribers. But this is still a great way to get started and can help to bring your content to the top of search lists, which will help you out down the road.

There are a few different characterizations that you will find when you work on a traffic video. Some of these include

- Massive reach: these videos are going to have a very high count of viewers to help you get people to your channel.
- The audience that you bring in will be undefined, wide, and sporadic. This can bring in some people but a lot of times it will not bring too many viewers permanently.
- Short length: these videos usually won't be more than seven minutes long.
- High amount of likes,
- High amount of shares
- Lots of comments
- Low conversion rate to channel subscribers, but it can help you to get some more of the likes that you need later on.

So let's talk about some of the different types of traffic videos that you are able to try out in order to get people into your channel and looking at your content.

Viral videos

These types of videos are going to include some short clips that can end up getting tens of millions of views. This is usually because followers will share the videos on social media and other places. They will usually be unique so that they catch the attention of others and it increases the number of shares. It will also be a standalone video, which means there will not be other videos that go in this series.

The whole purpose of going with this kind of video is to get as much attention as possible and to promote sharing throughout the community. They don't really reach a specific demographic either but will appeal to a lot of different people through social media so you get as many views as possible.

There are a variety of topics that you are able to pick from for creating your viral videos. Some of the topics that work well include:

- Celebrities that are in unexpected situations
- Fights
- Accidents
- Spoof sketches
- Song covers
- Animal videos
- Pranks.

Trending videos

Another type of video that you can use to help promote your YouTube channel is trending videos. These are the videos that will be about current hot topics of trending topics throughout the world or in the media. These will also be standalone videos and they are meant to give a unique interest in social media in the hopes of reaching millions of people with just one video. Of course, this type of video is also going to be broad in terms of the audience that you reach, and there won't be a specific type of demographic.

There are a lot of great trending topics that you can use in these videos, you just need to watch the news and make sure that you keep up to date. Some of the topics that you can use for your videos include sports highlights, festivals after a movie, explaining new technology, movie trailers, and political elections.

General interest video

These videos are going to be on a topic that has a wide amount of interest so that most social media users would want to take a look at it. These won't be shared as much as some of the other options, but they will still get quite a bit of view because of direct searches. Sometimes they are known as Unintentional Virals.

Some of the topics that you can place in one of these general interest videos include tutorials, reactions, social experiments, and product reviews. They should provide some kind of information and value to your customers or the viewers so that you still get quite a few people viewing the information.

Collaboration videos

You will find that collaboration videos can be successful as well, but they will work in a different way compared to the other categories. In these videos, there will be a few different YouTubers who will come together in the same video, but they are all able to present their own content within that video. When each collaborator is done, each YouTuber who was in the video will share it on their personal channel, helping to cross-promote and reach a much larger audience.

To work on a collaboration video, you will need to find other channels who are similar to yours so that you can target the right users and share a message that is similar to all channels. This is much more targeted compared to some of the other options so you are more likely to get a higher conversion rate.

So how do you get one of these collaborations to work? You first need to make sure that you are showing value to the other people who would join in on the video. You should go through and find a few channels that have a similar content and amount of subscribers before getting started. Let them know that you enjoy their videos, that you have been watching them for a bit of time and that you find that their message is captivating.

Once you have made some contact, you are able to explain how collaboration is able to help both of you reach a bigger audience, get new users, and then expand out both of your channels. Remember that this is not just about you; there has to be some value between you and the other channels or you will not be able to get the results that you want.

Picking out the type of video that you want to use is sometimes the biggest challenge of getting your channel up and running. You have to pick out the type of video that would work the best and come up with a catchy idea that will get people to look at your channel and hopefully start to get some more likes and even more subscribers that will grow your business. This is going to be a great way to get started on your channel, but remember that there are other things that you have to work on as well.

Once the original viral video is up and running, you will need to work on creating some of the other videos that you want to have on your channel. These can be about your service and product and will help to bring some more of the targeted viewers that you would like to have, but the viral video can be a good way to help rank your channel and helps you to see results.

Chapter 3: Understanding Your Audience

In the past chapter, we spent some time talking about one of the first things that you should do in order to attract some new users to your channel. The viral video is one of the best ways to get this done, but we still need to move on a bit more. The next task is to engage your viewers, the ones who found the channel in the first place and find a way to make them fall in love with your content. These are going to be your loyal customers, the ones that you will be able to upsell your services or products to later on. This is going to be the underlying process that will define your marketing on YouTube.

So the goal here is to produce content that is going to engage your audience. You need to be able to develop a thorough and deep understanding of who is in your target audience and what these people value. Before we begin though, there are two essential requirements that you need to keep in mind. When you are looking for an audience you must remember:

- The audience needs to have some interest in the subject or the theme of your videos.
- Your audience has to be active on YouTube

Now you will be able to identify your audience on YouTube. You have to remember that anyone you go after needs to fit into the two requirements that we listed above. If you have never spent much time working on marketing in the past, it may be hard to figure out how to pick out the right audience so that you can make some sales off your audience.

Before you start out on any of the videos that you want to create or you design your YouTube channel. You need to go through and answer these questions. These will help you to reach the right people and not waste all of the time and energy on reaching the wrong people. You should look back at the answers to these questions anytime that you are uncertain about what is going on or if you are sending out the right message to your customers. The five questions that you need to ask about your audience includes:

- How old are they? This can include whether they are teenagers or adults and even an age range if that helps.
- Where do these people live? Are they in a different time zone that will affect the time you post videos or are there any language barriers.
- Are they men or women?
- How do these people spend their day? Are they students, do they work, do they have families, and what is important to them?
- Why do these people go to YouTube for? How often do they go onto YouTube? Do they like to look for specific information when they are on YouTube or are they just passing time?

You will find that working with YouTube analytics, which will be discussed a bit more later on in this book, can be a great tool to help you pick out your viewers and learn more about them. Thanks to the fact that Google took over YouTube, you are now able to get details about the statistics of your viewers. In fact, you will be able to go through and see precise information about your viewers, and even more information about the audience as it grows. Or example, you are able to look through and see what type of information and content is going to appeal more to the women in your group.

If you have been in business for some time, you are going to be able to use some of the marketing information that you have used in the past. Your demographics can be similar on YouTube as they are on other social media channels so some of the work has been done for you. Of course, you have to remember that this social media is much different than some of the other sites. This one is going to rely just on videos, without copy and other words, so you may have to make some changes to reach your customers a bit better.

For those who are just beginning their process of marketing at all, you need to make sure that you do this analysis of your customers anyway. How are you supposed to make sure that you are marketing to the right people, rather than wasting your time and energy, no matter what type of marketing campaign that you are working on?

Knowing your audience is so important. You want to make sure that you are creating some great videos so that you reach your target audience and you don't waste your time and energy. By using the five questions above and asking as many other questions about your customers as possible, you will be able to get as much information in order as possible to create fantastic videos and make the sale.

Chapter 4: Provide Value to Your Audience That They Can't Get Anywhere Else

The next part of this journey that you need to work on is how to provide value to your customers. It is not enough to just make a few videos and hope that people will like them. These videos need to be able to provide some sort of value to your customers, to solve a problem for them, to entertain them, or do something else. Just spouting out information about your product is not going to be enough to help keep the viewers around.

If you are interested in getting millions of people to look at your content, you need to make sure that the content is high in quality. The videos need to be way better than the competition, and there is a lot of competition that you will have to go against. If you want to make sure that you can attract some new viewers and keep your viewers around, you need to make sure that the videos are not only high quality but the content needs to provide value as well.

Value is something that you are going to hear around the marketing industry all the time, but very few people understand what this means. From a high-level perspective, it can be defined pretty easily. Basically, this value means that your audience is going to attribute a level of importance, worth, and usefulness to your content. However, it is going to be hard to figure out the exact value that your audience place on the video and content that you upload, especially since this industry is completely digital.

Let's look at an example of this. The Fail videos have become really popular throughout the web. These are basically stunted attempts that end up failing in unexpected ways and can lead to the person getting harmed quite a bit from the accident. FailArmy is a popular channel that has over 12 million subscribers.

But the real question here is how can you describe why people like these kinds of videos. The viewers are going to watch any content that is bringing them value and it is your role as the marketer of your company to identify the value of these videos and then maximize its delivery to you viewers. So why are the Fail videos so popular? They are not that high quality, they are definitely not original and they aren't that unique

There is an article that is found in Adweek took the time to discuss the Fail videos and why people like them so much. There are three factors that are discussed including the Ego stroke, the element of surprise, and the element of disbelief. If you want to launch a channel that is similar to the topics of fail videos, you will need to carry out a lot of research on these three elements so that you can add them into your videos and add in more engagement.

Figuring out what your viewer's value is really difficult. You are not able to meet the people who are watching your videos and you have to be able to figure out what these people like, what they do in their free time, what they enjoy or find interesting, and so much more. However, if you would like to see sales of your products, you have to be able to understand the value to your viewers.

From some of the other topics that we have discussed in this book, you should already have a good understanding of who your target audience is. If you don't already have this organized and figured out, you need to go through and do this right now before going any further. You need to have a good appreciation and idea of some features including their age ranges, their gender, the way they browse the internet, their lifestyle habits, and more. These insights are going to be really useful when it is time for you to understand what is going to be valuable to your customers when making your videos

In order to really develop this understanding of your audience, you can use the approach below:

Step 1: Assess the competition

When you first get started on your new YouTube channel, or any new business or marketing avenue for that matter, the first thing that you should do is take a look at your competition. It doesn't matter what you are trying to sell, there are going to be some sort of competition, or another channel, that you are going with on YouTube.

Having competition is important because this shows that there are market and audiences that are already around for your content. It is much easier for you to fill a market need than to try and create a new one. There are many different types of competition that you need to work with. The direct competition will be the people who are selling a product like yours or very similar. If you are selling jewelry, these would be the other people who sell jewelry as well.

But there will also be the indirect competition and you cannot forget about these people either. If you sell hamburgers and French fries, you will also want to compete with the grocery store, taco places, and other places to eat. Each company is going to have both direct and indirect competition so learning who these people are can really help you to make higher quality and more on target videos than your competition.

You should look at both the large and the small competitors within your field. The smaller ones are who you will work with right away, the focus you should have right now. The larger ones you can tackle later when you start to gain some steam.

To start, you should look at five of the small and five of the large channels that have similar objectives to you. For each of them, you need to pick out three parts of their channel that you really like. You can pick the behind-the-scenes cuts, the high-quality videos, the topics and more. Once you are done writing this down for all of them, it is time to go through and write down three aspects of the channels that you don't really like. Then on each of these points, you need to write down information on how you can solve the issue in your own channel.

While you are going through all of this information, you always need to think about why people are watching these videos? What are these viewers trying to get out of these videos? You can take some time to look at some of the comments because these will provide a lot of insight into how people like these videos. Remember that you should use the positives from your competition, but learn from the mistakes that they have.

Step 2: Refine and improve your value proposition list

In the past step, you were in charge of developing a list to describe why users are attracted to your competitor's channel. However, if you go through and copy the competition all the time, you are never going to see success. Instead, you need to work on improving it. You must be able to differentiate yourself in some way so that you can steal more market share and provide content that has better value.

In order to do this, you need to refine the value proposition list as described in the steps below:

- Compare the value proposition to the target audience profile you developed. Can you optimize any of these aspects to the gender, habits, and age range of your target audience?
- Always play to your own strengths. Do you or anyone on your team possess unique skills that are you are able to use? For example, if you are really good at Photoshopping, you can do this to make some really good videos.
- Produce content: once you are done with your value proposition, which you adopted in the previous step, now it is time to produce and add in some new launch videos on your channel.
- Evaluate: as you add some new videos on your site, you are going to start to get some more feedback. You can take this information and start it all over again. There are going to be times when you will experience some criticism, but it is important to not run from this information, but instead, go straight towards it and try to make some improvements. Yes, there will be times

when the feedback is not all that useful, but other times when it could help you make big changes that will help you out.

One of the steps that you should work on is to isolate why some of your audience is positive to some of your videos and why they respond negatively to others. Once you come up with a theory, it is time to test the market. You can then start a new video that will address the customer feedback before going through the new response. Again, you will still get negative and positive feedback on the video (this will always happen because not everyone will like what you have to say), you can check out this new feedback and see if some new changes need to be done.

Continuous improvement is so important to help you see some of the results that you want. The companies that are dominating the market are the ones who always take a look at the feedback that you see on your videos and then you can make changes as needed.

Remember, in order to have a channel that is successful on YouTube, you have to first produce some content that is fantastic. But it is only one of the factors that you need to have come together to get the successful channel. Having high-quality videos can help you to attract some customers, but you need to have patience, learn how to engage your viewers, consistency, advertisement campaigns, and marketing in order to get the success that you want.

Chapter 5: Tips and Strategies That Work

As we spent some time discussing earlier in this book, you need to take some time to know who is in your target audience, understand what they will value, and then be able to provide this to the right people. This is all so important for helping you engage your audience. However, it is important for you to remember that YouTube is a platform for sharing videos and it is going to rely on communication and on graphics, which means your content isn't the only thing that you should concentrate on.

There are a lot of different details that need to come into play when designing your videos. Just sitting in front of the camera and talking for a bit is not going to do the trick. Some of these include:

Graphics and appearance of the channel homepage

When viewers go to watch one of the videos that you post and they like it, it is likely that these people are going to visit your homepage. The branding and the graphics will be one of the first things that they notice, so they need to make a powerful impact. While there are a few different types of graphics that you can place on your homepage, but the two components that are the most important include:

The profile picture: this is going to be the image that is the most visible on your whole channel. It is going to appear in the videos and in all of the comments that you end up posting.

Depending on the type of the business that you run, this could be a headshot of you or a company logo.

Banner picture: the banner picture is important as well. This banner picture is going to be a large one that is right in the background of your channel page. You want to make sure that this picture is of high-quality and that it is going to catch the attention of your viewers, helping to introduce them to the products or the subjects that you are promoting.

If you don't really have any experience with doing graphic design, it is a good idea to hire someone who can help you get this done. These graphics will be some of the first things that people notice when they go to your channel, so you want them to look nice. You will be able to find a few good designers to work with if you just search for a bit online. If you need some ideas of how your graphics should look, consider looking on some other channels to figure out what looks nice.

Banner video

Another thing that you need to work on is the banner video this will be the very first video that people will see when they come to your channel. You can have some fun with this kind of video, but you should make sure that it explains a bit about you, that it talks about your hopes for the channel, and even includes a bit of history about your business.

You do need to put some effort into this video because it needs to be one of your most engaging videos. It can only be a few minutes long, but it needs to be enough to convince someone who may have never heard about you in the past to like your videos and stick around. This needs to be a video that provides value to them and sell yourself.

Playlist and video arrangement

The playlist that you have on your channel can be a great way to attract new customers, but it does need to have some good groupings and the topics should be clear. You should have a structure that is effective or the channel. To start, you should write out a list of three or four topics that you think the viewers may enjoy, and then work to create your playlists around these subjects.

You do not want to end up with too many playlists when you first get started, so be careful when planning these out. You can add more of these later on, but as a beginner with just a few videos posted, it is best to start with just a few to keep things more organized. These are helpful because it is going to let a viewer know what your channel is all about right from the beginning and you are able to solve a problem for them this way, making things easier.

Engage right with the viewers.

No matter what type of product you are designing, you need to make sure that you and your viewers are working on a personal relationship. Your customers are interested in purchasing products from people that they know and trust so you need to work on this kind of relationship through the videos that you are creating.

There are a few strategies that you are able to work with in order to achieve a direct and strong emotional connection with all of your viewers. The first one is to learn how to speak right to your viewers and thank them for taking the time to look at your channel. The second thing that you are able to do is to be active in your comment section. While you may not be able to take the time to respond to everyone who is commenting on your videos, but making an effort and responding to as many of these as you can make a big difference.

As you can see, high-quality videos are so important when it comes to creating a great video to use on YouTube, there are some other factors that are so important to helping you to get views. You can make as many videos as you would like and post them, but without the other factors, you will get no views.

Chapter 6: Upselling a Product or Service with the Conversion Video

So far in this book, we have spent some time talking about how to make up your viral video so that you can get people into your channel. Then we moved over to working on some videos that are going to connect with your viewers, things that will solve a problem and provide them with a bit of value in the process so they stick around. Now we are going to move onto the step that you need in order to start making money from your YouTube channel!

Once you have been able to funnel some more viewers to go to your channel and you have learned how to keep them engaged, it is time to learn how to sell the service or product that you have available. This one can be exciting because all of that hard work you have put into the rest of the process in order to start making the money that you would like.

Now it is time to convince the viewers that they need to purchase your service or product. In most cases, the viewers on your channel don't already have a need for the product. Otherwise, they would have just gone out and gotten the product already on their own. It is your job to show them how the product or the service is going to bring them value so they make the purchase.

One of the most effective ways that you are able to convince your viewers to go for your service or product is to use Conversion Videos. These types of videos are important because they are meant to convert the audience that you already have into customers. These videos can be longer in length, sometimes up to two hours although most companies will not make their videos that long.

It is important to remember that these videos are only going to appeal to a specific niche in your audience. You will not receive as many views on the video as you did and the comments and shares will be lower as well, but this is not a big deal. If you did the other steps correctly, you will still get customers to look at the video and they are more likely to be the ones you need to make the sale.

There are a few factors that you are going to be able to find in your conversion videos Some of the features that are found in these types of videos include:

- Longer video length that is often between five minutes and two hours.
- Low amount of shares
- Low amount of comments
- Low amount of likes
- A specific and refined audience
- Restricted reach that is pretty much limited to the subscribers you already have, so it is important to make sure that you have plenty of these in place before you start.

Now that we know a bit about these conversion videos, it is time to discuss some of the popular and most effective types of conversion videos.

Knowledge video

These videos are great because you will demonstrate an outstanding, complete, and extensive knowledge of a given topic. Your job on here is to show that you are an expert in your field, that you are the person that everyone else should go to if they want to learn more about this particular topic.

Through these videos, you are going to market out your knowledge in this field. This is going to help you to sell books, plans, advice, or something else. Often these are steeply priced so being able to show the subscribers that you have the value of working with you can be a big deal. Some of the examples of what can be shown in these knowledge videos include:

- Presentations and talks
- Personal opinions and podcasts
- How-to
- Tutorials
- Tips

Demonstration video

The next thing that you can work on is the demonstration video. This type of video is when you will show the viewers exactly how the product or service you are selling is going to work. Remember that the main challenge that you face when marketing a product is to show how your product or service will provide value to your customers. When you do a demonstration video, you are able to demonstrate to your customers how valuable the product is.

In these videos, it is more important for you to focus on the benefits that the product and service providers, rather than the way that the product works. Of course, you can show some of how the product works, but it is more important to show some of the benefits of this product. Some of the examples of how you are able to do this are with personal experience, product review, documentary, gameplay, testimonials, portfolio work, and client transformation.

Call-for-support video request

In these kinds of videos, you are going to need to work on the emotional bond that you have been building with your viewers. Even though the viewer may not necessarily need your product right now, you will find that these videos are perfect for getting them to make a purchase a form of appreciation for you and your videos. This strategy is only going to work out well for you if you have a lot of engagement from your viewers or an audience of millions.

You do not want to start with these conversion videos right off the bat. Your customers need to build up a relationship with you before they will make a purchase and if you just try to get them to make a purchase with the first video that you make, you are going to end up with some trouble making the sales that you would like.

But, if you start out with some relationship building videos first, videos that provide some sort of benefit to your customers and keeps them coming back for more, it is easier to use these conversion videos once your audience levels are up, so you can get the results that you want. You may be excited to start earning a lot of money right away when you are on YouTube, but if you don't appeal to your target market and give them some value ahead of time, you are putting in a lot of work for nothing.

Chapter 7: Promoting Your Videos

Now, we have spent quite a bit of time in this book talking about how you can create videos and some of the different options that you can choose when you want to bring in more customers to your channel. So now that you have a great video, how are you going to promote your videos so that the most customers will see this content. You can have some fantastic videos and content to share with others, but without some promotion, you are going to end up with a lot of effort and nothing to show for it.

There are times, especially when you are just getting started on a new channel, where you are not going to be satisfied with how many views your video is able to get organically. Organic views are basically the number of users who are able to see and look at your videos without having to use paid advertising to help you out. For some people who haven't started with social media and online marketing, the idea of paying money for one of these marketing campaigns can seem a little bit overwhelming and expensive. The good news is that these campaigns can be really easy to do and if you create the right types of videos, it will easily pay for itself.

Although you may not realize it when you are on the other side of things, the channels that are the most successful on YouTube are going to be the ones that use paid ad campaigns. But they don't just do a few little campaigns here or there; instead, they will do these on a big scale. For instance, some of the larger music videos are able to acquire their first two or more million through a big ad campaign that happens right after they release the video. Because of this and a large amount of traffic that happens right after the video has been released, the algorithm for YouTube is going to see this as an important video and will promote it. This means that YouTube will feature this video on their homepage and it can quickly go viral.

This means that using ads on YouTube is so important, but as a beginner, where are you supposed to start. This chapter is going to take some time to talk about which platforms you are able to use for advertising, what objectives you can achieve with each one, and even how to set up an ad campaign to help you get started.

The best tool in AdWords

AdWords is considered one of the best and largest advertisement services available online today. It is a service that is created and owned by Google and it earns more than $40 billion a year. Thanks to the amount of user information that Google has in their possession, AdWords will allow you to refine your target audience using interests, gender, and age. And after Google acquired YouTube, they also changed up AdWords so that it works with videos as well.

After being used for decades by many online advertisers to help reach their target customers, AdWords for Videos was developed to be used easily and to be accessible to everyone who would like to use it. All you need to do is create the ad that you would like to use, define the target audience, and then select your budgeting options. Once all of this is done, AdWords for Video will work to make sure that your ad is in front of any user that has looked at the similar content and will help you get more views and subscribers.

The question that most people have after all this information is how much does it cost to run a campaign with AdWords. You will be surprised at how inexpensive it is to place your content in front of an audience who is targeted, meaning an audience who is interested in the information and will likely follow your channel.

The nice thing about AdWords for Video is that you are only going to pay for the video once someone watches it. You won't have to pay just because someone sees the title of the video or anything else, but only when they actually take some time to look over your video. On top of that, if you are on a limited budget to get started, you are able to set a price per view or even a daily budget to help you stay on track.

If you find that the campaign is not working as well as you would like, or if it is doing better than you had hoped, you will be able to stop or modify your campaign at any time. You don't need to give up a notice to make this happen. Remember that both AdWords and YouTube offer sections for analytics so that you are able to see how successful all of your marketing campaigns are going to be, with a lot of precision to help you decide whether the campaign is doing what you would like.

Before you get started with any type of marketing campaign, much less one that you use with AdWords for your videos, you need to have an approach set up ahead of time and this approach needs to have some clearly defined goals to help you succeed. Another thing that you will enjoy about working with AdWords for Videos is that it is going to provide you with some settings that can help you to match the objectives of your campaign. There are quite a few of these available, but one of the three options below are often the best ones for a beginner to get started off:

- I want to reach more people: if you want to do a campaign that will reach a lot of people and funnel these people into your channel, AdWords is able to help you out with this. To help with objective, you will need to work on promoting a traffic video like the ones that we discussed earlier in this book.
- I want to increase engagement: if you want to do a campaign that will help to increase the engagement on your videos, you will find that there are some other tools that are more effective, but you can do a few things with AdWords. If you want to use AdWords for this, it is best to focus on the content, channel presentation, and quality before you move to doing this.
- I want to increase conversions: AdWords is one of the best tools to use for increasing conversions on your videos. Conversions are the number of people who end up purchasing the service or product that you promote on YouTube. You can work on increasing your audience members before starting and then promote these with an Upsell Video.

You will find that AdWords is going to make things so much easier. You will not be limited to just the subscribers that you are able to organically get into your videos. With the help of AdWords, you will be able to reach anyone who has expressed some interest in your services or products directly. Of course, most of these users will have no idea of who you are and that emotional connection is not going to be there. This sometimes results in a lower rate of conversion. But if you place the Upsell Video in front of enough people you will usually see an increase in your sales.

Advertising with Facebook

Although working with AdWords for Video is a great platform to use to advertise your channel, using Facebook is another channel that is available to help you out. Due to the large amount of personal information that people seem to share on Facebook, you will be able to effectively target audiences that you want to work with and show them your message.

If you are brand new to the marketing world and you want to keep your budget under control, working with Facebook is a great option for you. Many people see Facebook is one of the cheapest and most effective platforms for you to use for online advertisement. This is a good way to share some of the videos that you want to promote and get them to spread virally among your friends and others. You may need to do an advertising campaign to help spread this out beyond the few people that you know, but it can be a cost-effective way to bring people back to your YouTube channel.

Working with various social media platforms is one of the best ways that you can help to promote your video outside of YouTube. While that is outside the scope of this book, it can make a big difference in how many people will take a look at your videos and go back to your channel.

Chapter 8: How to Create an AdWords Campaign

We spent some time talking about AdWords for Video on the last chapter and how it can be one of the best tools to help you get your content out to your potentials so that you can make money from your work. But if you have never worked on an AdWords campaign, it can be a little bit scary to get started on the first one. This chapter is going to split up the steps that you need in order to create your first campaign with the help of AdWords for Video. This process is really simple, even for people who are not used to doing an online campaign for their company.

The first step is to get onto the account for Google AdWords for Video This is going to help you to create your very own AdWords campaign. You just need to go to the website **www.adwords.google.com/videos**. You can use the credentials for your YouTube or Google account to get started. Then pick out your time zone and the currency you would prefer to use.

Once you have had the time to create your own AdWords account, it is time to link up your channel from YouTube and then create a brand new campaign. Before you are able to create this campaign, you need to make sure that you link together the AdWords account with your YouTube account. This makes it easier for you to select the videos you want to work with directly and it will provide you with campaign analytics that is more detailed. You can also use this to insert some call-to-action buttons if you would like. To start, you need to click on the "Linked YouTube Accounts" which is located right on the bottom left corner of the screen to have this happen.

Once you are on that link, it is time to create a new campaign. You need to look for the button that is called "All Video Campaigns". You will be able to find this on the top left corner of the screen. When you have found that button, you will be able to choose "+New Video Campaign" to get started with the first campaign.

You will want to select a few parameters that you would like to have on your campaign to make it look nice the first parameter that you should set for this campaign is what you would like to call the campaign. Make it something catchy and easy to remember so you can find it later on. And the second parameter that you need to set is the daily budget you would like to spend. This can help you to keep things under control and that your budget won't reach to the sky.

While you are setting up the parameters that you want to use, it is time to work on defining the location and languages that come with your ad. You can first start by refining your audience and who you would like to reach you can choose which cities the audience lives in and even the country if you would like to expand out the audience a little bit. And of course, make sure to pick out the language that will reach your target audience the most.

Once some of the parameters are set for your ad, it is time to pick out the video that you would like to show up when the ad is displayed. In order to get this started, you need to look for the button that says "select video" and then search through the list of available videos to find the one that you want to display. You can also do this by using the URL link, the channel name, or the keywords to make this easier. You will want to make sure that the video you are promoting is one that will capture the attention of your customers and bring them in to get more views. Use some of the tips in the first few chapters to figure out which one you would like to use.

When you are working with AdWords for Video, you will find that this program is going to use TrueView. This is a marketing model that is only going to charge the advertiser when a viewer has actively watched your video ad. There are a few formats that you are able to choose when you create your TrueView ads, and these are going to determine where the ad is going to be displayed on the page on YouTube. It is important to pick the one that is best for you to ensure that you will be able to get the results that you want. The four formats that you can choose for TrueView include:

- In-search: this is where the ads are going to appear on the search page for YouTube. Viewers will be able to see the ad, either next to or above the search returns on YouTube when they start to search for content that is related to your video. You will only need to pay when someone clicks on the ad and then watches your video.
- In-display: with this option, your ads are going to appear right next to the videos on the watch page on YouTube. Viewers will be able to click on your display ad in order to watch the video that is in the ad or on a YouTube watch or channel page. This one is also where you will only pay when someone clicks on the ad and then watches the video.
- In-stream: this is when the ads are going to play pre-, mid-, or post-roll on one of the YouTube partner videos that can be of any length. With these, you can place a whole ad, but the viewers do have the option to skip

away from your video after five seconds are done. You will only have to pay for the ad when someone watches the entirety of the ad or after 30 seconds are over.

- In-slate: this is when the ads are going to play before a partner video on YouTube. Usually, the videos that the ad will play before will last over ten minutes. Before the video plays, the viewers will be able to choose to watch one out of three ads, or they will be able to watch regular commercial breaks throughout the video. You will only need to pay when someone clicks on the ad and starts to watch the video.

As you can see, there are different amounts of exposure that you will be able to get when you choose each of the options. Some will not get as many views as others but will be cheaper than the other options or you can get more views and pay a bit more. It is all about what you would like to do to target your customers and how much your budget is to do this.

Once you have chosen the type of ad that you would like to do from the formats that were above, it is time to define how you would like the ad to appear to your viewers. The main features that you need to spend time defining include the text of the headline, the description text, the destination URL, the thumbnail image, and the name of the ad (this last part is only going to be seen by you and the viewers will never see it).

At this point, it is time for you to set your own target bid. This is the section where you are going to be able to define the most that you will be willing to pay for each add. You will notice that this is called the CPV or the Cost Per View. Remember, that in most platforms online and social media, ad space is going to be assigned based on a bidding strategy. If you end up sending out bids that are too low, you will not be able to win any space for your ad.

There are a few different bidding settings that you will be able to pick out when it comes to this process. You are able to choose between the basic bidding settings or the advanced settings. The advanced bidding will make it easier for you to make modifications to the bid for each of those four ad locations we talked about before, whereas, in the basic bidding, you are going to maintain the same maximum bid no matter which ad location you are using.

Next, you will need to name and then save the target audience you would like to work with. This is not something that the viewers are going to be able to see, but it can help you to keep things organized in this campaign and will be nice for your future campaigns. From here, you will be able to proceed and then define who the viewers of your ad campaign are, also known as defining your target audience.

You will be asked during this process to pick out some keywords as well. You want to pick out some keywords that are relevant to the users you are working with. This makes it easier for them to find you when they do a search similar to what you are offering. If you are having trouble coming up with the keywords that you would like to use, you should just do a quick search for the interests that your audience has. You can also use the service known as "Get Targeting Suggestions" from YouTube so that you can pick out the audience you want to work with and then see the keywords that are the most relevant.

It is possible to use the same kind of process in order to select targeting keywords that are negative. These are going to represent the users that you do not, under any circumstances, want to advertise to. For instance, if you are working on a channel that really promotes barbecue meat, you may want to pick out a negative target keyword for the word "vegetarian."

And finally, you need to make sure that in this last section you are providing the right payment information to AdWords. Your ads will never be published on YouTube if you do not provide this payment information because YouTube wants to get paid when you get views.

Working with AdWords is not a complicated process, even though we did take a few pages to go through it all You will see that there are a lot of suggestions and modifications that you can make, but this is all meant to make things easier for you to target the right people. Take the time to consider the best placement for your ads on YouTube, the right keywords, the video you want to use, and so on, and you are more likely to get the results that you want to form these targeted campaigns with AdWords.

Chapter 9: Tracking Your Performance with the Help of YouTube Analytics

Once you are done creating your campaign with all of the tools that we have talked about so far in this book, it is time to move on to figuring out whether the campaign is working or not. No marketer wants to get into the game and hope that things will work out for them, but never really having a way to find out whether they are reaching the right audience or not. This is where YouTube Analytics can come into play.

YouTube Analytics is a tool that will provide you with a lot of information on the success and the growth of your audience, videos, and the whole of your YouTube channel. If you have never used something like YouTube Analytics before, you are going to be shocked at all of the information that is provided inside of this tool once you get started. For example, it is possible to use this tool to find out exactly how your audience reached your YouTube channel, right down to the link that they clicked on to get to you. This is just one of the cool things that you are able to do with YouTube Analytics.

How to access YouTube Analytics

While YouTube Analytics is a great tool to use, you have to make sure that you are able to access it before you are able to use it to your advantage. On some social media platforms, you will find that it is difficult to access the analytics tools that they have set up. For example, you are only able to get access to the analytics that is available on Twitter if you pay for marketing campaigns through them. The good news is that getting onto YouTube Analytics is free and pretty simple.

The first step that you need to do is log onto your personal YouTube channel. Once you are there, you just need to follow the link **www.youtube.com/analytics**. After you have had time to open up this page, you should search for the tool bar. There should be an Analytics tab that you can click on before being sent over to the overview section.

The overview screen is a good place to start. It is going to provide you with a summary of the most important relevant data that is on your channel. You can just glance through this page and get some of the general trends of your channel. There are going to be quite a few items that will be listed in this overview screen. Some of these include:

- View reports: this is the place where you should go if you would like to figure out the number of views that you have received over time. You can also use it to see the source of all these reports to target your advertising better.
- Demographics report: with this tab, you will get a good breakdown of your audience. You are going to use this data to refine the profile for the target audience that we made earlier in the book. Some of the most relevant metrics that you will find include age breakdown, playback location, and gender distribution.
- Traffic sources report: this is a really important report that you will be able to use. It is going to help you to learn exactly how a user found your video, which can be so important when you want to grow your channel. For example, if an external blog featured your video, you will be able to see how many of your views came from that particular source.
- Audience retention report: this is going to be the most important data to engage your audience. It is going to

show you how well the audience was engaged during the whole video. Often engagement is going to fall off as the video goes on unless something amazing is going on during your video. It is important to figure out where you are losing the audience and use this as a method to improve your video.

After you get started with a new video or a new ad campaign, you should give it a little bit of time to get out there and for people to take a look at it. You will not be able to get very good analytics half an hour after you post a brand-new video. The good news is that you will be able to get some good updates on a regular basis if you are patient and let the analytics do their job.

It is a good idea to go through this analytics on a regular basis so that you can get things set up and ready to go in a timely manner. There is so much information that you will be able to get from this analytics and you can use this information to figure out the best topics to work with, the best places to advertise, and so much more. Remember that your videos need to provide some form of value to the viewers so if you see that engagement is dropping off or you are not getting the number of views that you would like, it may be time to switch things up a little bit. Analytics will help you to get this done so you can see the results in no time.

Conclusion

Thank for making it through to the end of this book, let's hope it was informative and able to provide you with all of the tools you need to achieve your goals whatever they may be.

The next step is to figure out exactly how you want to sell yourself on YouTube. The type of product that you have for sale is going to make a huge difference in this, so be prepared and working on that first video, the one that is going to draw people in can often be one of the best places for you to get started. Many people are too worried about making videos that are going to just sell their products, but they forget that the customers want to feel a bond with the seller first, long before they look at any of the products that are for sale.

This book has all the information that you need to get started with success on your own YouTube channel. It doesn't matter what kind of product or service you are trying to sell, you want to make sure that you are following the steps that we outlined. From understanding how to make your first video to providing value to your customers, to a promotion of the videos, and even to promoting your own product over time, you will gain all the insight that you need to see results with this unique form of marketing.

YouTube is not a marketing channel that you want to turn down. There are so many things that you will be able to do with this channel and it is so effective at helping you to form that relationship with your potential customers. When you are ready to get started with using YouTube for your marketing needs, make sure to read through this book and learn everything that you need to know!

THANK YOU! :)

Finally, if you found this book useful in any way, a review on Amazon is always appreciated!

Check Out My Other Books

Below you'll find some of my other popular books that are popular on Amazon and Kindle as well. Simply click on the links below to check them out. Alternatively, you can visit my author page on Amazon to see other work done by me.

www.amazon.com/Mark-Smith/e/B01JZ91Q5E/ref=ntt_dp_epwbk_0

www.ingramcontent.com/pod-product-compliance
Lightning Source LLC
Chambersburg PA
CBHW071520210326
41597CB00018B/2826